SO, YOU WANT TO BE A SENSITIVITY READER?

PATRICE WILLIAMS MARKS

Circa

Copyright © 2018-2019 by Patrice Williams Marks

All rights reserved.

No part of this book may be reproduced in any form or by any electronic or mechanical means, including information storage and retrieval systems, without written permission from the author, except for the use of brief quotations in a book review.

THE FREE "SENSITIVITY READING" COMPANION COURSE

To help guide you, consider taking our **free 7-day course** which includes examples, assignments and more. Reading this book is your *first* step to success. The free course is the *second*. **Click on the button below for instant access. See you on the inside!**

https://freecourse.sensitivityreviews.com

https://freecourse.sensitivityreviews.com

FAN OF HOW-TO BOOKS? WANT EARLY ACCESS?

I am a fan of sharing information. That's why I've written a Hacking Kickstarter series as well as this book on Sensitivity Reading as a business.

If you'd like to gain early access to new releases *(and receive free gifts as a thank you)* simply click on the button below.

https://www.patricewilliamsmarks.com/readers

https://www.patricewilliamsmarks.com/readers/

Dedicated to all avid readers, authors, writers and bloggers who place no limits on becoming a successful entrepreneur.

JOIN MY LAUNCH TEAM

If you enjoy reading my books, consider joining my official launch team for new releases.

Launch Team members will be invited to my exclusive private community and have their names added to future ebook releases as a thank you. (You would also receive a free ebook and possible paperback copy).

For more details, go to: https://goo.gl/x7meuD

(Launch team member names to be added here soon with next update).

1
WHAT IS A SENSITIVITY READER?

So what is a Sensitivity Reader, anyway?
A Sensitivity Reader is someone who has a writing or editing background; (or simply an avid reader) with extensive personal experiences that they use to draw upon when they review projects submitted to them

others call this authenticity

for bias, racism, or unintentional stereotypes.

(BTW: If you're not offended by the above Dove ad, you should not be a Sensitivity Reader).

Sensitivity Readers are not regular editors or censors. They do not proof, look for holes in stories, or re-write or delete content. In fact, all projects given to Sensitivity Readers are given voluntarily. The Sensitivity Reader simply reads for what they consider to be offensive content, misrepresentation or stereotypes, and points it out. The **author of the content chooses** whether to use their suggestions or not.

The children's book, A Birthday Cake For

So, You Want to be a Sensitivity Reader? | 3

George Washington, was pulled by Scholastic for showing a "happy slave" baking a cake for one of our founding fathers. The authors romanticized slavery and ignored the fact that Hercules, the baker, was ripped away from his family and put into forced labor for George Washington. Hercules tried to escape many times, yet the book recklessly conveyed to children that Hercules and his daughter, Delia were "happy slaves." Several African-American Sensitivity Readers would have caught this right away and could have helped them avoid the public outcry and boycott of this book which cost Scholastic a bundle. *(Note: Hercules did eventually escape from slavery, but had to leave his daughter behind. They conveniently left that part out.)*

So who can be a Sensitivity Reader? If you belong to a marginalized group and have experienced being viewed as a stereotype, faced bias or racism, then you have a mandatory tool in order to become a Sensitivity Reader. Some of these groups include: *the disabled, little people, African-Americans, Hispanics, Asians, Indians, Anti Semitism, LGBTQ, Native Americans, Muslims, Middle-Eastern, the obese, are in an interracial relationship*; just to name a few.

There are several more must-have skills needed in order to offer this service to book publishers, authors, the gaming community, marketing agencies, etc.

2

WHO CAN BE A SENSITIVITY READER?

If you're an author, writer, or avid reader, you may already have the right tools to get started working as a sensitivity reader.

Which specific niche(s) would you be qualified for? Are you a member of the LGBTQ community? Are you Hispanic, Indian, obese, African-American, Muslim, a Little Person, Asian? Do you have experience with mental illness, foster care, etc.?

Hone in on your niche(s) and be very specific about what types of projects you're qualified to review.

Then offer "free" Sensitivity Reads to

fellow authors, friends of friends, or acquaintances.

Once you've done a handful and you have happy, satisfied clients, ask them for testimonials.

With testimonials in hand, position yourself online through your website and social media as a Sensitivity Reader in your specific niche(s).

Sensitivity readers charge according to their experience and skill set. But please note and tell future clients: Sensitivity readers are not editors in the normal sense.

They do not proof, rewrite, or find holes in stories. They simply read in order to determine whether bias, stereotypes, racism or assumptions are present, and offer possible solutions.

Sensitivity readers are needed in book publishing, gaming, film, television, marketing, and other industries.

I was on Reddit last month on a gaming thread. There was an indie game creator looking for African-American gamers to beta-test his project prior to release.

He had several characters within the

game who were black and had them speaking heavy slang.

Thankfully he understood that someone who was actually black and played games should take a peek before release.

Sensitivity reading can be both fulfilling and lucrative.

If you fall into a much-needed niche and would like to provide a valuable, in-demand service, consider becoming a sensitivity reader.

3

WHO COULD USE A SENSITIVITY READER, AND IS IT CENSORSHIP?

In 2016, Scholastic pulled the children's book, *A Birthday Cake For George Washington*, after outrage from what some considered "whitewashing" of the history of slavery.

The book showed "happy slaves" making a cake for George Washington. To those of us with ancestors who lived through that period of time–my father's grandmother was a freed slave–it was not only hurtful but insulting.

We know that Scholastic (and the authors of the book) had no intention of insulting or whitewashing slavery, but nevertheless, they did just that. How? By writing about a culture they knew little about, and filling in the holes with assumptions though their own limited lenses.

As writers, we all "fill in the holes." I have. But it has always been after extensive research.

What could they have done differently?

Hired several African-American Sensitivity Readers during the first draft phase of the book.

What could they have done differently?

Hired several African-American Sensitivity Readers during the first draft phase of the book.

What exactly is a Sensitivity Reader, and how could s/he have helped?

A Sensitivity Reader is someone who specializes in a specific niche (African-American, Muslim, Physically Challenged, LGBTQ, Little People, the obese, etc.) and is a part of the specific marginalized community that the author is writing about. The Sensitivity Reader thoroughly reads over the material for bias, stereotypes, offensiveness, lack of understanding, etc. and creates a report for the client outlining their thoughts, why they feel something may be a problem, and offering possible solutions.

Will a Sensitivity Reader censor the work?

The **client makes the final decision** whether to make the changes suggested, make only a few changes, or keep the project as is.

Some writers believe that they should be

So, You Want to be a Sensitivity Reader? | 11

free to write whatever they want and not be scrutinized. That is true to a point. No one is forced to hire a Sensitivity Reader. But authors who understand that their point of view is only one point of view and that others exist, may want to hire a Sensitivity Reader.

If you grew up in the Hamptons, but want to write about a family in the Chicago projects, you should not rely on how you "think" the characters would act, speak or live (from what you've seen on television or the news), but have someone who has lived, or lives that life, as a sounding board.

Sensitivity Reading is a service, another tool in the writer's belt. Authors who write diverse books, but do not have first-hand experience with the people they are writing about, can make use of a Sensitivity Reader in the niche they require.

Does a project need more than one Sensitivity Reader?

Possibly. If you are writing about more than one marginalized group, and you are not part of those groups, then you would do well to hire Sensitivity Readers who specialize in each group.

4

DO YOU HAVE THE BACKGROUND TO BECOME A SENSITIVITY READER?

So Let's Delve Further Into What Exactly a Sensitivity Read Is.

According to Writerunboxed author **Natalia Sylvester**," *a sensitivity read is an evaluation of a manuscript, usually, one that touches upon characters and experiences of a marginalized group of people, that is performed by someone within that group to bring attention to potential inaccuracies, biases, and reinforcements of harmful stereotypes. Much like one might ask a cardiologist to read their story about a cardiologist for accuracy, a sensitivity read helps ensure that the portrayal of characters and worlds unknown to the author ring true. But more* *than that, it helps authors better yield the immense power and responsibility of their words."*

Are You Qualified to Be a Sensitivity Reader?

So you've bought this book so you're pretty sure you're qualified to be a Sensitivity Reader. That's good. Knowing yourself, your experiences and background will make you a sought-after Sensitivity Reader. But let's still delve into what makes a great Sensitivity Reader.

• You belong to a marginalized group (such as African-American, Native American, Asian, Hispanic, Little People, the obese/plus size, Muslim, Middle-Eastern, the disabled, etc.) and have personally experienced negative bias, racism, stereotyping, bigotry or misrepresentation.

• You are a writer, (professional or not) and love expressing yourself that way

• You are already used to helping people; from writing reviews on Amazon, Yelp, to community volunteerism

• You have a firm grasp of the English language

do you?

- You *may* have experience with a second language (both reading and writing)
- You are able to formulate your thoughts clearly and concisely
- You are a hard worker and are willing to work towards your goals
- You are organized
- You understand social media and have *at least one* active social media account
- You have or are willing to create a professional presence online
- You follow-up on a timely fashion
- You have integrity
- You want to be a Sensitivity Reader to help people, not wag your finger at them

What Are Your Accomplishments?

Your accomplishments are considered your strengths. Use your strengths to hone in on your niches. How?

Success in any field can be found by drilling down your audience — and not enlarging it too soon. Identify your strengths, and replicate your accomplishments. Think in terms of templates and the savings associated with reusing versus reinventing the wheel, and you will quickly see

So, You Want to be a Sensitivity Reader? | 15

the return on your investment from your niche.

So, by focusing specifically on micro-niches, you will build a reputation as the go-to person. As you carve out that niche, you will enjoy the benefit of creating relationships with potential customers.

What is a mico-niche?

It is a niche within a niche. Let's say you're a Native-American. Then let's say you're a member of the Blackfoot Tribe. That is a niche within a niche. They are easy to find. Simply google possible niche's and "auto-complete" will pull up "micro-niches."

Here is an example. I've decided that my niche is, "*African-American women*." I google, "*African-American women*," and this is what is suggested to me:

So Google has suggested our micro-niches for us:

- Black History Heroins
- Women's Rights
- Black women who changed the world

You get the idea. Play around with this to come up with your own unique list. here is another way to find micro-niches.

Wikipedia.org.

Simply go to their home page and type in a niche. This is what happened when I typed in "*the disabled.*"

Wikipedia suggested:
- Disabled Veterans
- Disabled Sports
- Ableism

Have fun honing in on your niche!

Further Education:
Further education is not simply referring to whether you have a college degree or not, but "life" education. Have you taken weekend classes in a favorite subject? Have you done volunteer work and learned how to landscape or put up drywall? I bet you can come up with a ton of experiences and skills that make you unique.

I recently gave a Sensitivity Read for a writer who had an African-American female lead who had been in Foster Care most her life. I was uniquely qualified for this read as I am African-American, and I am also a Foster Mom to infants. I was able to give her insights into the character that she would not have had if she simply had an African-American Sensitivity Reader without Foster Care experience.

Discovering Your Niche From Leveraging Your Education & Accomplishments:
Discovering your niche generally means that you find a place where you fit in and feel comfortable because you have a passion for that area/subject, and experience.

Certainly, you want to do your due diligence in selecting a viable niche for your Sensitivity Read business, but it's better to get up and running than to wait around for the perfect moment. That way, you can test out ideas, enter the market sooner and learn from your successes and failures. Also, if your first niche doesn't take off, you can always take what you've learned from previous attempts and move forward with new niches.

If you're struggling to decide, here are a few ways to discover yours:

- How do you spend your free time?
- What magazines do you read?
- What newsletters do you subscribe to?
- Do you belong to any social clubs?

Answer these questions, and come up with a list of 5 niches you are qualified to read for.

5

HOW DO YOU BECOME A SENSITIVITY READER?

You've heard a little something about Sensitivity Reading, and you've asked yourself, "Just how do I become a Sensitivity Reader?"

Good question.

There is a growing need for Sensitivity Readers as authors, publishers, gaming companies, marketing agencies include people of color and/or marginalized individuals in their projects and want to make sure they are not misrepresenting a group or race, unintentionally.

Definition of a Sensitivity Reader, according to Writers In the Margins: A **sensitivity reader** *reads through a manuscript for issues of* *representation and for instances of bias on the page.*

Sensitivity Readers have the following characteristics:

. ***They want to make a difference in this world:*** They've seen books, commercials, films, tweets, or the like that are disrespectful to groups of people and are surprised that no one else noticed. They want to genuinely help people who seek out their advice. They believe that they can make a difference.

. **They love to read:** They are avid readers and may even belong to a book club. They look forward to the next adventure or romance that unfolds within the pages of the new book they ordered from Amazon. They spend time at the library checking out new books, finding a cozy nook to read a book there.

. **Belong to a marginalized group:** They have to have a special niche that they have experience with and will focus on. (*A few marginalized groups include: African-Americans, Asians, Hispanics, Native Americans, Jewish, Muslim, Middle Eastern, the disabled, the mentally ill, foster parents, foster children, interracial* *relationships, LGBTQ, the obese, plus-size, lived in poor communities, etc.)*

. **Want to work from home:** They may have a full time job outside the home, but want to subsidize their income. They may be a stay-at-home mom or dad looking to start a business with very little money, make their own hours and create a sizable first or second income.

. **Have personal experience to draw upon:** They have accessed their skills and know they have something special to offer. They have personally experienced racism, bias, or the like, and will use those experiences to help others in their writing.

. **They understand that they are not censoring anything:** That people come to them willingly and seek their advice as someone with knowledge and experience. They know that they only give advice from personal experience, and that it is up to the content creator whether they make changes to their project or not. They also understand that they are just another optional tool in the writer's belt.

So the job of a Sensitivity Reader is to only accept projects that fall within their niche of experience, read through the manuscript, note instances they think need to be addressed, and offer solutions and other resources.

If you've read through all six points and have nodded your head yes, then you could be a Sensitivity Reader.

6
WHAT CAN/SHOULD YOU REVIEW AS A PAID SENSITIVITY READER?

Should You Accept All Projects?
If you've taken the quick quiz to the module, then you know the answer is a resounding NO! Although you are a member of a marginalized group and have personally faced racism, bias, or misrepresentation, you are not uniquely qualified to read for EVERY character within your group or niche.

Why? Because remember, you must have personal experiences to draw upon.

Let's say for example, you are a member of the LGBTQ community, but you have not told a soul; not even your parents or siblings. Your closest friends suspect, but figure if you want them to know, you would share it with them. Your life has not been touched by hardships felt by others in the community. You don't participate in marches, you do not have friends in that community who know your story; in fact, most people just see you as an average caucasian guy.

But now you've decided that your niche is the LGBTQ because a lot of authors have these characters in their books; especially the Young Adult genre, and you want to jump on the hot trend now. You figure you can do the reads on the side using a "pen name," and keep yourself anonymous.

Are you qualified to read for projects that feature characters from LGBTQ community?

No, you are not.

I hope that is plain enough. In fact, if this person decided to set up shop as a Sensitivity Reader for the LGBTQ community, he would be doing a great disservice to this profession and for the LGBTQ community. Why? Because he has zero experience with that community, despite the fact that he is gay. He has not lived the life of a gay person, had their experiences, both good and bad. So how can this person effectively represent the community? He cannot. He would be "guessing," and perhaps perpetuating stereotypes of the community based on his opinions alone. And that is exactly what a Sensitivity Reader reads for; pointing out misinformation and offering solutions.

So, before you accept a project, ask yourself these questions:

1. Is it a niche I'm qualified to read for?

2. Do I have personal experiences to draw upon?

3. Will I be reviewing based on my own experiences, (and not from what I've read, seen in the media, or have been told)?

4. Am I a good fit for the project?

If you've answered yes to all 4 questions, then you are qualified for the read.

WHAT DOES A SENSITIVITY REVIEW COVER?

As a Sensitivity Reader...
...your experience, your opinion, your knowledge matters. Clients who seek you out and hire you, want to make use of your vast experience within your chosen niches.

Before you are hired to complete a Sensitivity Review, you should be extremely clear on what you can/will offer to your clients, and communicate that to them before you begin work.

What Sensitivity Reviews Cover:
- Read for misrepresentations of a mar-

So, You Want to be a Sensitivity Reader? | 27

ginalized group or race
- Read for bias against a marginalized group or race
- Read for racism/bigotry against a marginalized group or race
- Read for stereotypes against a marginalized group or race
- Review character descriptions, actions (example: only describing the skin color of minorities and not the white characters)
- Review dialog of characters (example: do you have all minority characters speaking in slang?)
- Review character backgrounds (example: are all your Mexican characters illegals?)
- Review for historical accuracy (example: do you have all African-American characters in the 1900's as former slaves?)
- Read for overall concept

What Sensitivity Reviews Do NOT Cover:
- Belittling the author/writer
- Editing/Proofing in any form
- Rewriting
- Suggestions for holes in the story
- Mandatory corrections

- Censorship
- Removal of any negative characteristics of a group or race (not all minority or marginalized groups have to be portrayed as good)

8

HOW MUCH CAN YOU MAKE?

Setting the price for your Sensitivity Reads can be a challenge.

To be successful you must understand many different aspects of this business, where you want to be in the future and what has worked for others in the past.

Let's take a look at Sensitivity Readers for full-length novels. I'll give you two scenarios:

Marcy has published seven novels on her own with steady sales. She prides herself on being a one-person-band when it comes to writing, marketing and selling her novels. She transitioned into a Sensitivity Reader three years ago after helping out fellow authors with Asian characters; pointing out stereotypes or bias they mistakenly used. She started her business through research and honed in on her niches. She now has a steady stream of clients, charging each novel she reviews between $500 and $750; depending on the length. She only accepts two novels a week in order to continue her own writing career, and give her client's projects the attention they deserve.

Randy is not a novelist, but loves to read. In fact, he reads 3-4 new books a month. He belongs to three different book clubs and considers himself a bookworm. He just learned about Sensitivity Reading as a business two months ago, and has decided to give it a try. He's always given his opinions on Amazon, Google and Yelp, and gets many "helpful" upvotes, so this business came naturally to him. Randy joined a Reddit group for book lovers and introduced himself and offered his services for free to five people with projects under ten-thousand words. He informed the group that his niches included the disabled, cannabis users and African-American men. Randy has completed the free projects with glowing testimonials and just signed up his second paid project; a full novel. Randy was still getting his footing and only charged $250 for the novel review.

As you can see from the two examples, both are Sensitivity Readers but charge quite different than each other. Marcy is a more established brand, while Randy is an up-in-comer. Marcy makes more money now, but, if Randy continues to get more reviews under his belt, he could easily move into Marcy's pricing.

> **Factors that influence price**
>
> **DON'T BE AFRAID TO LOSE**
> *don't take a job out of desperation*
>
> *Try: don't lower your price "just because"*

Your Pricing:
Deciding on your price does not have to be hard and fast; it can be flowing and evolve with you. But remember these rules:
- **DON'T** charge too little and cheapen your service
- **DON'T** charge too much before your experience & expertise warrant the higher costs
- **DON'T** lower your price if someone

says "they can't afford it and asks for a discount"
- **DO** re-evaluate your costs with every few reviews
- **DO** value your time and expertise
- **DO** provide value no matter how much your charge

NOTE: Most Sensitivity Readers have clients who re-write their projects based on the suggestions the reader made and will ask them to do a re-assessment.

Some Sensitivity Readers do this for free, but only comment in generalities, while others specifically go over all the changes which is an additional fee you can charge.

Consider These Factors When Setting Your Prices:
Start with Your Direct Costs:
Ask yourself:
- How much time does it take to service a customer?
- Costs for software?
- Should I calculate research time into the project?

Take Into Account ALL of Your Expenses:

Once you understand your direct costs, you need to look at the other costs for running your Sensitivity Reading business. Covering your overhead and other fixed costs is important if this is a full-time job for you.

Ignoring Your Competition's Pricing:

There are many Sensitivity Readers charging different prices. Choosing your price *"because it is what your competitor charges"* is a bad idea. Why? Although it is important to know what other Sensitivity Readers are charging to stay in the ballpark; don't mirror them exactly. You should just have an idea what the marketplace is charging in order to explain why your prices are more or less.

If your client understands why they should hire you (*your expertise in a needed niche*), the price will not be a significant factor in their decision to hire you. Being cheaper doesn't mean you will win every time; only that you'll get a reputation as the "*cheap*" Sensitivity Reader they can nickel and dime.

Evaluate Past Sensitivity Reads:

Evaluate your past projects, then ask yourself:

- Did I work more hours than I anticipated?
- How much did I make per hour (counting hours you worked on project and divide by amount you charged)?
- Did I price my services too low?
- Did I make money on the project, or lose?

By knowing the marketplace and charging according to your expertise, you can't fail at pricing your services correctly.

9

HOW I USED A SENSITIVITY READER FOR MY EPIC SCREENPLAY

How I Used a Sensitivity Reader to Review My Epic Screenplay 15 Years Ago

About fifteen years ago I wrote a script based on real people; a famous British explorer, Samuel Baker, who found his future wife, a Hungarian aristocrat, on a slave block in Bulgaria. He bought her freedom. The two eventually fell in love and set out on an adventure to find the source of the Nile.

I could only do so much research online, so I joined the Royal Geographical Society and traveled to London to read original manuscripts written by Samuel Baker. I also had the pleasure of meeting descendants of Florence Baker in Salisbury England. They shared a diary written by her, along with little known facts and nuances about Florence that I could have only gotten from them.

After completing the script, I forwarded to them to check for accuracy. They caught a few missteps and I chose to make the changes.

I didn't know it then, but that could have been considered a *Sensitivity Read*.

So what is a Sensitivity Reader, anyway?

A Sensitivity Reader is someone who has a writing or editing background; (or simply an avid reader) with extensive personal experiences that they use to draw upon when they review projects submitted to them for misrepresentations, bias, racism, or unintentional stereotypes.

Sensitivity Readers are not regular editors or censors.

They do not proof, look for holes in stories, or re-write or delete content. In fact, all projects given to Sensitivity Readers are given voluntarily. The Sensitivity Reader simply reads for what they consider to be offensive content, misrepresentation or stereotypes, and points it out. The author of the content chooses whether to use their suggestions or not.

A Sensitivity Reader is also someone who specializes in a specific niche (African-American, Muslim, Physically Challenged, LGBTQ, Little People, the obese, etc.) and are part of the specific marginalized community that the author is writing about. The Sensitivity Reader thoroughly reads over the material for bias, stereotypes, offensiveness, lack of understanding, etc. and creates a report for the client outlining their thoughts, why they feel something may be a problem, and offering possible solutions.

Will a Sensitivity Reader censor the work?

The client makes the final decision whether to make the changes suggested, make only a few changes, or keep the project as is.

Some writers believe that they should be free to write whatever they want and not be scrutinized. That is true to a point. No one is forced to hire a Sensitivity Reader. But authors who understand that their point of view is only one point of view and that others exist, may want to hire a Sensitivity Reader.

If you grew up in the Hamptons, but want to write about a family in the Chicago projects, you should not rely on how you "think" the characters would act, speak or live (from what you've seen on television or the news), but have someone who has lived, or lives that life, as a sounding board.

Sensitivity Reading is a service, another tool in the writer's belt.

So, You Want to be a Sensitivity Reader? | 39

Authors who write diverse books, but do not have first-hand experience with the people they are writing about, can make use of a Sensitivity Reader in the niche they require.

10

DO YOU NEED A FORMAL CONTRACT WHEN WORKING AS A SENSITIVITY READER?

Do You Need a Formal Contract?
(Note: I am not an attorney. This is simply advice born from personal experience. You may choose to have your own attorney draw up an agreement for you).

Finally, a "paid" client reaches out to you. You're excited! You understand what they need and you can deliver it. You decide on a price, send a Paypal invoice; they pay, then you get started. Right?

WRONG!

Let's step back in this progress.

1. You've promoted your business
2. A potential client reaches out to you

3. You interview them and see the material and decide the project is right for you

4. ~~You send them a Paypal invoice~~ ==> ***You send them a contract to sign***

You might be thinking, "Why would I want a contract with a client?" **<u>TO PROTECT YOURSELF AND THEM.</u>** You don't want your livelihood to be at risk, or get the dreaded, "*chargeback*" notice, (where they treat you as guilty by debiting your account ***before*** the investigation begins).

How many cases have you seen on *The People's Court*, or *Judge Judy* where two people didn't have a contract in writing and where each assumed something totally different? And how many may have worked hard and never received a penny? Quite a few, I'm sorry to say

That's not going to be you.

Creating a contract that **both** of your sign means you *value your work*. If you don't value your work, other people won't value it either. So it's best to have an agreement, written out with specific details that both of you sign. If there is something in the agreement that the client wants tweaked, then you have an opportunity to address their issue(s) prior to you beginning work.

Below are Contract Must-Haves

CONTACT INFORMATION: It sounds basic, but getting the client's name and address, email and cell number gives you the ability to contact them by other means if their email bounces and/or they don't answer their phone.

Also, if you ever have to serve that person with papers for nonpayment on your project (*if they do a chargeback and win*), you have a way to serve them. <u>Remember, **NEVER** begin work without **full payment.**</u>

Having a contract also protects your client and gives them peace of mind. If you don't deliver on your Sensitivity Review, they also have a copy of the contract with your information.

CONTRACT SCOPE: The contract scope breaks down all the responsibilities of the Sensitivity Reviewer, what is included in the review, etc. It also includes a delivery date, word count, etc. ***Always include word count*** because I have discovered that authors/clients always UNDERESTIMATE the word count. (My last client told me the project was 80k words, when, in fact, it was 92k words. After doing the word count on my own, I informed them that my price was contingent on the 80k word count and gave them a new price. They had the option of paying the additional fee, or, having me stop at 80k).

AVOID SCOPE CROSSED BOUNDARIES: By having a clear understanding of what you will and will not be providing, you avoid the client "asking" for additional services that were not included in the scope of the contract. If they do ask, and it's something you provide, then alter the contract to include the new service and add an additional fee. They will need to sign and initial the new changes. (*Example: They would like for you to post an Amazon review of their book. If you don't mind doing this, simply add this to the contract as an addendum, along with an additional fee*).

PAYMENT INFORMATION: One of the most important sections of the contract is the payment section. This is where you put your price, word count, payment in full before beginning work notice, payment due date, etc.

ARBITRATION, LEGALESE, REPROCUSSIONS OUTLINED: In this section you outline what happens if either party fails to abide by the contract. This protects both of you. You should have specific repercussions outlined, along with a dollar amount assigned to the offenses.

I also outline when and if a refund is on the table. If I have begun work, I have a no-refund policy. If I have not begun work, I do refunds if I am asked within a specific period of time. You decide what is best for your business.

As far as arbitration goes, adding that section is up to you. I do not have it in my contract because I am very specific on payment and refunds. You may, however, decide to add an arbitration clause.

DISCLAIMER: Always include a disclaimer at the end of your contract explaining that your review does not guarantee or absolve them of any negative criticism for the project.

This is my disclaimer:

Client understands that having an objective outside eye review their work may catch their biases, but a Sensitivity Reader cannot guarantee that they will catch everything, and that it will be free from bias. Hiring a Sensitivity Reader does not absolve your work from possible criticism, nor does the Sensitivity Reader speak for every person who falls within their scope of work. Hiring a Sensitivity Reader is not an en-

dorsement of any project. It is also a good idea to hire more than one Sensitivity Reader.

SIGNATURES: Now that you've included everything that you need in your contract, it's time to sign! I suggest you follow these steps in order to be as professional as possible, while making the process easy on you and your clients.

Register for an account with HelloSign.com - This service is free to use for 3 contracts a month. If you go over that, they have cheap month-to-month rates. HelloSign allows you to upload your pdf contract, designate how many people need to sign the agreement, where they are to add information, where to date, where to sign. *See screencast below*.

While sending a contract to a client might seem intimidating or too much... believe me, it is not! You will thank me later after it has saved your butt a few times! And as you get a few contracts under your belt, it will come very natural to you. You will also come across as very professional to your

So, You Want to be a Sensitivity Reader?

clients. It instills trust and respect; a great way to begin a relationship.

Want an **Email Contract** instead? I don't recommend it. Going back and forth between multiple emails would be confusing with no way to sign a finalized agreement. It's simply a recipe for disaster.

11

F.A.Q.

How do you get started as a Sensitivity Reader?

If you're an author, writer or avid reader, you may already have the right tools to get started. Which specific niche(s) would you be qualified for? *Are you a member of the LGBTQ community? Are you Hispanic, Indian, obese, African-American, Muslim, a Little Person, Asian, have experience with mental illness, foster care, etc.?* Hone in on your niche(s) and be very specific about what types of projects you're qualified to review. Then offer "free" Sensitivity Reads to fellow authors, friends of friends, or acquaintances. Once you've done a handful and you have happy, satisfied clients, ask them for testimonials. With testimonials in hand, position yourself online through your website and social media as a Sensitivity Reader in your specific niche(s).

Are Sensitivity Readers paid?
Yes, they are. You could consider them "diversity editors." Sensitivity Readers charge according to their experience and skill set. But please note: Sensitivity Readers are not editors in the normal sense. They do not proof, re-write, or find holes in stories. They simply read in order to determine if bias, stereotypes, racism or assumptions are present, and offer possible solutions.

I was on Reddit last month on a gaming thread. There was an indie game creator looking for African-American gamers to beta test his project prior to release. He had several characters within the game who were black, and had them speaking heavy slang. Thankfully he understood that someone who was actually black and played games should take a peak before release.

Sensitivity Readers are needed in the

book publishing industry, gaming, film, television, marketing and more. Sensitivity Reading can be both fulfilling and lucrative.

Does a project need more than one Sensitivity Reader?

Possibly. If you are writing about more than one marginalized group, and you are not part of those groups, then you would do well to hire Sensitivity Readers who specialize in each group.

Have other questions? Email me at admin@sensitivityreviews.com and ask.

12

READY TO TO LAUNCH YOUR NEW BUSINESS AS A PAID SENSITIVITY READER?

Ready to become a PAID Sensitivity Reader but *need a roadmap*? You're in luck.

I've created an extensive online course in Sensitivity Reading just for people like you.

You not only will learn the basics, but also how to put together a business site in 2 hours, how to find clients, how to do a Sensitivity Read, learn how much money you can make, how to get testimonials *BEFORE* your first Sensitivity Read, along with a sample legal contract to use when taking on clients with free software suggestions/links.

> *Note: Some graduated students are eligible to be included in our database of Sensitivity Readers for more referral business.*

The course is broken down into modules with work assignments, videos, fun quizzes, downloads, examples and a private facebook group for students.

All students also receive access to me personally through a weekly live meeting.

You will learn absolutely everything you need in order to start your own Sensitivity Reading business, from start to finish.

- *Avoid: Trial and error black holes*
- *Avoid:* Costly and time-consuming mistakes
- *Avoid:* Normal pitfalls in starting a new business
- *Start:* An in-demand business with people looking for your skill set in your unique niche
- *Learn* from a working, in-demand Sensitivity Reader (who is also an

author, screenwriter and founder of a non-profit charity)
- *Earn:* Start earning money in as little as two month

Below, you'll find details on the course. *Don't feel overwhelmed* as we take the course one-module-per-week. If you have questions, get stuck, or have feedback, you can reach out at any time.

The course is very easy to follow and has lots of videos, quizzes and content with bite-size pieces.

Here are comments from past students:

Anne Balad - Entrepreneur

As an Asian woman, I've seen several ad campaigns targeted towards minorities, which were biased. I wanted to do something about it, and discovered Sensitivity Reviews is a real thing. This is the only course I've discovered online on the subject and was excited to take the courses. Now, I not only see the potential of making fantastic income as a sensitivity reader, but feel good about providing this type of service. Thank you, Patrice for giving me everything I need to start my own business.

Kareem Mohammed Maize - Rockstar Entrepreneurial Starters

> I recent signed up for her Sensitivity Reading courses with Patrice which changed my life and my worldview. Now I am making a good side income while helping to expose bias in advertising that I didn't even realize existed. This is especially important to me since I am from middle eastern descent and most of my family is Muslim. Thank you so

much Patrice for helping me make a good income while making the world more aware of its unconscious biases towards ethnic minorities.

Check out the COURSE CURRICULUM:

Sensitivity Reading 201: Complete Blueprint For Launching Your Review Service Course (Standard)

Module 1: Welcome!
Lesson 1: Welcome Video & Definition of Sensitivity Reader
Lesson 2: Are You Qualified to be a Sensitivity Reader? Nailing Your Niche
Lesson 3: Deciding Types of Projects You Want to Review (And Shouldn't)
Lesson 4: Download Workbook Assignment

. . .

Module 2: Your Presence Online
Lesson 1: Quickstart Guide (No Website Needed)
Lesson 2: Quiz - Module 2
Lesson 3: Download Workbook Assignment -

Module 3: You the Expert
Lesson 1: Video - Yes, You're The Expert
Lesson 2: Blogging As An Expert in Your Field
Lesson 3: Download Workbook Assignment -

Module 4: If You Build It...
Lesson 1: Gathering Testimonials Before Your First Paid Customer
Lesson 2: Guest Articles on Industry Blogs
Lesson 3: Partner With Fellow Students Via Private Facebook Group
Lesson 4: Quiz - Module 4
Lesson 5: Download Workbook Assignment -

Module 5: Setting Your Prices
Lesson 1: Industry Average Pricing & Establishing Your Fees
Lesson 2: Offer Satisfaction Guarantee
Lesson 3: Download Workbook Assignment -

Module 6: Writing a Sensitivity Review From Start to Finish
Lesson 1: What a Sensitivity Review Covers (And Doesn't)
Lesson 2: What Do You Do First?
Lesson 3: Sample Sensitivity Review
Lesson 4: Quiz - Module 6
Lesson 5: Now It's Your Turn - Complete Your First Sensitivity Review
Lesson 6: Download Workbook Assignment

Module 7: Written Contracts & Agreements
Lesson 1: Why Have a Contract?
Lesson 2: Sample Contract

Lesson 3: Download Workbook Assignment

Module 8: Your Roadmap: Passion. Patience. Perfection.
Lesson 1: Congrats Video!
Lesson 2: Roadmap: Passion and Patience and Perfection
Lesson 3: Download Workbook Assignment

Module 9: Additional Support
Lesson 1: Certification Option
Lesson 2: Make Money Sharing This Course With Others
Lesson 3: Download Workbook As One Complete Document (optional)
More info: https://sensitivityreviews.com/courses

13

FREE DOWNLOAD: PREPARING FOR YOUR BUSINESS

Download by clicking on image (**image may be on next page**) or going to: https://www.sensitivityreviews.com/wp-content/uploads/2018/05/Preparing-For-Your-Review-Service.pdf

So, You Want to be a Sensitivity Reader? | 61

Preparing For Your Review Service
SensitivityReviews.com

Starting any business requires a clear design process. Here is your roadmap:

Choose Niche
STEP 01
Be very specific. Choose a unique niche that makes you stand out from the crowd.

Web & Social Presence
STEP 02
Create a clean Landing Page on your blog & be crystal clear about who your customer is and how you solve their problems.

Socially Interact
STEP 03
Interact with your potential customers on social media without selling.

Offer Services
STEP 04
Where you see a need, offer your services.

The Delivery
STEP 05
Make an agreement and stick to it, delivering on time.

Patrice Williams Marks / SensitivityReviews.com

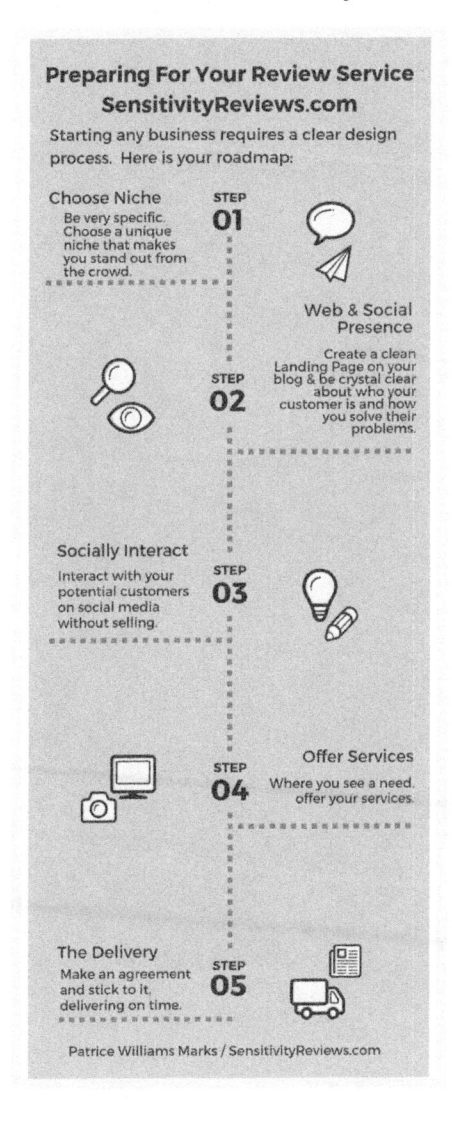

JOIN MY LAUNCH TEAM

If you enjoy reading my books, consider joining my official launch team for new releases.

Launch Team members will be invited to my exclusive private community and have their names added to future ebook releases as a thank you. (You would also receive a free ebook and possible paperback copy).

For more details, go to: https://goo.gl/x7meuD

(Launch team member names to be added here soon with next update).

14

WANT TO SHARE THIS COURSE WITH OTHERS?

Our affiliate program is free to join, it's easy to sign-up and requires no technical knowledge. Affiliate programs are common and offers SensitivityReviews.com another form of marketing.

Affiliates generate traffic and sales for our courses and other content, and in return, they receive a generous commission. (View our Terms and Conditions). Base commissions are 30%.

To read more or to sign up, CLICK HERE.

(https://www.sensitivityreviews.com/affiliate-home/)

ABOUT THE AUTHOR

JOIN SENSITIVITY REVIEWS MAILING LIST

Patrice Williams Marks is an author, Sensitivity Reader, founder of courses that teach Sensitivity Reading, founder of a non-profit charity, founder of several film festivals with diverse entries from filmmakers and writers. She also has a background in public relations, marketing, and journalism with an emphasis on research.

Reach Out:
www.SensitivityReviews.com

www.PatriceWilliamsMarks.com
admin@SensitivityReviews.com

Reviews welcome on all platforms.

Printed in Great Britain
by Amazon